ABT

FRIENDS
OF ACPL

W9-AFR-187

# Team Spirit

# THE BUFFALO BILLS

BY

MARK STEWART

Content Consultant
Jason Aikens
Collections Curator
The Professional Football Hall of Fame

NORWOOD HOUSE PRESS

CHICAGO, ILLINOIS

Norwood House Press
P.O. Box 316598
Chicago, Illinois 60631

For information regarding Norwood House Press, please visit our website at:
www.norwoodhousepress.com or call 866-565-2900.

PHOTO CREDITS:
All photos courtesy of AP Images—AP/Wide World Photos, Inc. except the following:
Topps, Inc. (16, 20, 21, 22, 29, 34 both, 35 top left and right, 36,
40 top and bottom left, 41 top and bottom right & 43);
John Klein (23 both); Author's Collection (26 & 37).
Special thanks to Topps, Inc.

Editor: Mike Kennedy
Associate Editor: Brian Fitzgerald
Designer: Ron Jaffe
Project Management: Black Book Partners, LLC.
Special thanks to: Frederick Piwko and Michael Radell

LIBRARY OF CONGRESS CATALOGING-IN-PUBLICATION DATA

Stewart, Mark, 1960-
  The Buffalo Bills / by Mark Stewart ; content consultant, Jason Aikens.
    p. cm. -- (Team spirit)
  Summary: "Presents the history, accomplishments and key personalities of
the Buffalo Bills football team. Includes timelines, quotes, maps, glossary
and websites"--Provided by publisher.
  Includes bibliographical references and index.
  ISBN-13: 978-1-59953-128-1 (lib. bdg. : alk. paper)
  ISBN-10: 1-59953-128-3 (lib. bdg. : alk. paper)
  1. Buffalo Bills (Football team)--History--Juvenile literature.  I. Aikens,
Jason.  II. Title.
GV956.B83S84 2008
796.332'640974797--dc22
                                                            2007008347

© 2008 by Norwood House Press.
All rights reserved.
No part of this book may be reproduced without written permission from the publisher.
•
The Buffalo Bills is a registered trademark of Buffalo Bills, Inc.
This publication is not affiliated with the Buffalo Bills, Buffalo Bills, Inc.,
The National Football League, or The National Football League Players Association.

Manufactured in the United States of America.

**COVER PHOTO:** Peerless Price and Nate Clements jump for joy after a
victory during the 2006 season.

# Table of Contents

SPORTS WORDS & VOCABULARY WORDS: In this book, you will find many words that are new to you. You may also see familiar words used in new ways. The glossary on page 46 gives the meanings of football words, as well as "everyday" words that have special football meanings. These words appear in **bold type** throughout the book. The glossary on page 47 gives the meanings of vocabulary words that are not related to football. They appear in ***bold italic type*** throughout the book.

# Meet the Bills

F ew **National Football League (NFL)** teams capture the spirit of their hometown the way the Buffalo Bills do. The city of Buffalo, in western New York State, is a place that prides itself on living life to the fullest. When times are good, every day is a celebration. When times are not so good, the people of Buffalo put their heads down and work twice as hard until things get better.

The Bills play football the same way. When they have a lead, they look for ways to send the crowd home happy. When they are behind, they come back one hard-fought yard at a time. Either way, they always give their fans a reason to rise from their seats and make a lot of noise.

This book tells the story of the Bills. Some of the best players in history have worn the Buffalo uniform, but the team is most dangerous when everyone on the field contributes. In their greatest victories and their most heartbreaking defeats, the Bills have played the only way they know how—as a team.

Terrence McGee is congratulated by Ryan Neufeld after returning a kickoff for a touchdown.

# Way Back When

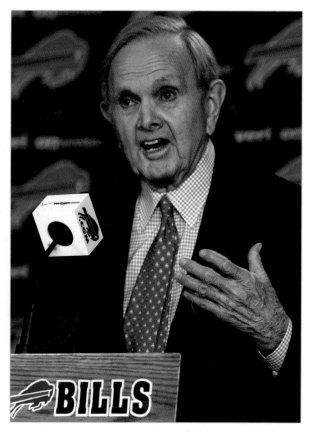

The Bills play in one of pro football's coldest cities. They almost began in one of its warmest. In 1959, a businessman named Ralph Wilson decided to buy a team in the new **American Football League (AFL)**. He wanted to put the club in Miami, Florida, but the city's leaders discouraged him. Wilson turned to a town that he knew would welcome a team with open arms—Buffalo.

In their early years, the Bills were led by coach Lou Saban and a smart and talented quarterback named Jack Kemp. Kemp's favorite receiver was Elbert Dubenion, who specialized in catching long passes. Buffalo had a strong running game powered by **lineman** Billy Shaw and running back Cookie Gilchrist. Tom Sestak and George Saimes led the defense.

**LEFT**: Ralph Wilson
**RIGHT**: Jack Kemp, Buffalo's leader during the 1960s.

In 1970, the Bills were one of 10 AFL teams to join the NFL. By then, they had football's most exciting player, O.J. Simpson. He was a swift and explosive running back who had the league's best **blockers** in front of him. Simpson was nicknamed the "Juice" and his offensive line was known as the "Electric Company." In 1973, Simpson became the first player in history to rush for more than 2,000 yards in a season.

Despite talented players like Simpson, Buffalo won just one **playoff game** between 1966 and 1987. The team had three great Joes during this period—Joe Ferguson, Joe DeLamielleure, and Joe Cribbs. However, the Bills could not compete against strong clubs such as the Miami Dolphins, Pittsburgh Steelers, and Oakland Raiders.

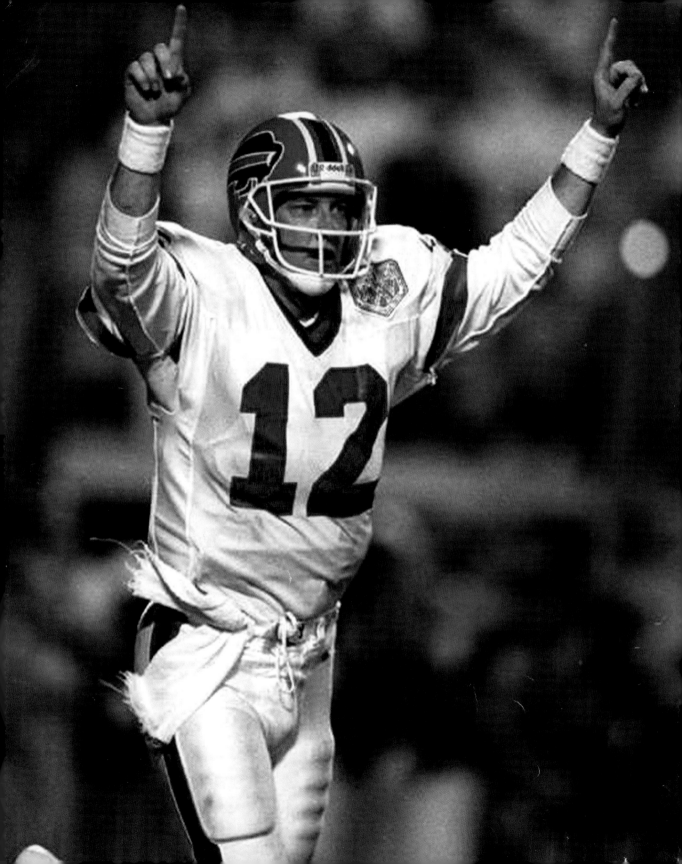

Buffalo's luck began to change when coach Marv Levy and quarterback Jim Kelly joined the team in 1986. Kelly was the perfect leader for the *hard-nosed* Bills. No passer in the NFL was tougher, and few could match Kelly's strong and accurate throwing arm. With help from running back Thurman Thomas and defensive stars Darryl Talley, Shane Conlan, Cornelius Bennett, and Bruce Smith, Buffalo played in the **Super Bowl** four years in a row during the 1990s.

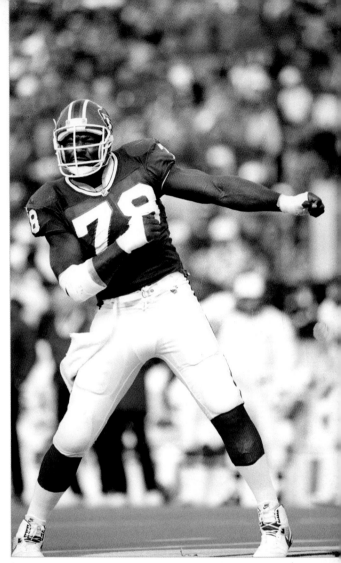

The Bills are fondly remembered for those great teams, but some fans would rather forget the Super Bowls. Buffalo lost all four. The team welcomed new stars in the years that followed, including Bryce Paup and Eric Moulds. As they entered the 21st century, the Bills were still searching for their first NFL Championship.

**LEFT**: Jim Kelly, Buffalo's leader on offense during the team's glory years in the 1990s. **ABOVE**: Bruce Smith celebrates a sack during the Bills' third run to the Super Bowl.

3 1833 05315 4057

# The Team Today

Keeping a competitive team on the field in the NFL can be a big challenge. As Buffalo's great stars of the 1990s faded, the Bills struggled to find good replacements. They rebuilt their team with trades and **draft picks**, always searching for a "diamond in the rough" while trying to rediscover their winning chemistry.

Among the talented newcomers to the Bills were quarterback J.P. Losman and receiver Lee Evans. Building around this core of talent, Buffalo started its journey back to the top of the **Eastern Division** of the **American Football Conference (AFC)**.

To get there, the team needs a top defense. The Bills have played for seven championships during their history, and each time it was their defense that led them to the big game. They have already started to follow their old *blueprint*, mixing exciting young stars such as Aaron Schobel and Terrence McGee with old pros such as Angelo Crowell.

J.P. Losman gets protection from his teammates to throw a pass. The Bills build their team around young stars who learn from the club's experienced players.

# Home Turf

From 1960 to 1972, the Bills played in War Memorial Stadium, an old ballpark built during the 1930s. In 1973, a new stadium was completed for the Bills. For many years, it was called Rich Stadium, after a local food company that helped *finance* the project. In 1998, the field was renamed Ralph Wilson Stadium, after the Bills' owner. It has been enlarged and modernized several times since then.

Although the stands at Ralph Wilson Stadium can be very chilly on winter days, Bills fans love to watch football there. The stadium features three *tiers* of blue and red seats, including sections with heated chairs and enclosed areas designed for comfortable viewing. The playing field is 50 feet below ground level, so fans in the upper deck do not have to climb too high.

## BY THE NUMBERS

- *There are 73,967 seats in the Bills' stadium.*
- *The Bills defeated the New York Jets 9–7 in the first regular-season game in their current stadium.*
- *In January 1991, the Bills beat the Oakland Raiders 51–3 in the first* **AFC Championship** *game played in their stadium.*
- *The Bills' first stadium was featured in the baseball movie* THE NATURAL.

A sunny Sunday is a welcome sight for fans at Ralph Wilson Stadium.

# Dressed for Success

When the Bills took the field for the first time in 1960, their team colors were bright blue, white, and silver. Their helmets were silver with blue numbers on the sides. In 1962, the Bills included red in their uniforms and changed their helmet color to white, with a standing red buffalo on the side. The team wore this design until 1974, when a modern-looking blue buffalo with a red streak took its place. During the 1980s, the Bills changed to red helmets. In 2002, they switched their uniform color to a darker shade of blue.

How did the Bills get their name? They borrowed it from Buffalo's old team in the **All-America Football Conference**. Owner Ralph Wilson loved the name Bills and saw no reason to change it—even though it has nothing to do with the city. "Bills" actually refers to "Buffalo Bill" Cody, a famous entertainer who traveled the country in the 1800s with his Wild West show.

O.J. Simpson models the Bills' home uniform from the late 1960s.

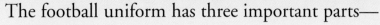

The football uniform has three important parts—

- Helmet
- Jersey
- Pants

Helmets used to be made out of leather, and they did not have facemasks—ouch! Today, helmets are made of super-strong plastic. The uniform top, or jersey, is made of thick fabric. It fits snugly around a player so that tacklers cannot grab it and pull him down. The pants come down just over the knees.

There is a lot more to a football uniform than what you see on the outside. Air can be pumped inside the helmet to give it a snug, padded fit. The jersey covers shoulder pads, and sometimes a rib protector called a flak jacket. The pants include pads that protect the hips, thighs, *tailbone*, and knees.

Football teams have two sets of uniforms—one dark and one light. This makes it easier to tell two teams apart on the field. Almost all teams wear their dark uniforms at home and their light ones on the road.

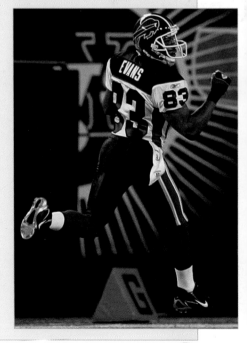

Lee Evans breaks free for a long gain in the Bills' 2006 road uniform.

# We Won!

In the early years of the American Football League, the scores were high and the games were wild. The Bills were the **exception** to this rule. They looked more like an NFL team. Buffalo had a defense that **overwhelmed** opponents and an offense that controlled the ball with a steady ground attack. In 1964, the Bills finished 12–2 to win the Eastern Division and earn a place in the **AFL Championship** game.

MIKE STRATTON  LINEBACKER BUFFALO BILLS

The Bills faced the San Diego Chargers and their star running back, Keith Lincoln. The first time the Chargers had the ball, Lincoln sliced through the Buffalo defense for a 38-yard gain. Moments later, San Diego scored to take a 7–0 lead. The next time the Chargers had the ball, Lincoln caught a short pass with Mike Stratton, the Bills' best linebacker, waiting for him. Stratton made a hard tackle, forcing Lincoln to leave the game. San Diego's offense struggled the rest of the day.

The Bills took a 13–7 lead in the first half on two **field goals** by Pete Gogolak and a touchdown run by Wray Carlton. In the final

period, Jack Kemp threw a 48-yard pass to Glenn Bass, who was tackled one yard short of the goal line. Kemp then scored the game's final touchdown on a **quarterback sneak**. The Bills, playing before a noisy home crowd, won 20–7 to become AFL champions.

One year later, the same two teams played for the title again, this time in San Diego. The game began as a tense defensive battle. By halftime, however, the Bills had taken a 14–0 lead. The key play was a 74-yard punt return by Butch Byrd for a touchdown.

The Bills surprised the Chargers in that game by lining up with two tight ends. They also confused San Diego with some creative defensive *strategies*. The Bills kept the Chargers from scoring in the second half, while Kemp guided the team on three time-consuming **drives**. Each one ended with a field goal by Gogolak. The final score was 23–0, as Buffalo celebrated its second title in a row.

**LEFT**: Mike Stratton, whose great tackle helped the Bills win their first title.
**ABOVE**: Lou Saban, Pete Gogolak, Jack Kemp, and Wray Carlton celebrate their 1964 AFL Championship.

The Bills played for the championship in 1966, but were beaten by the Kansas City Chiefs. A *merger* between the AFL and the NFL had just been announced, and the winner of the game was to play in the first Super Bowl. The Bills missed this chance and had to wait until the 1990 season before they reached the big game.

Starting that season, the team rewarded the patience of its fans by winning the AFC Championship four years in a row. Unfortunately, they lost in the Super Bowl each time—to the New York Giants, Washington Redskins, and Dallas Cowboys twice. The Bills led in three of these games, but fell short in their quest for a Super Bowl victory.

**LEFT**: Thurman Thomas runs against the Giants in Super Bowl XXV— Buffalo's first trip to football's greatest game.   **ABOVE**: James Lofton celebrates a touchdown during the 1991 playoffs.

# Go-To Guys

To be a true star in the NFL, you need more than fast feet and a big body. You have to be a "go-to guy"—someone the coach wants on the field at the end of a big game. Bills fans have had a lot to cheer about over the years, including these great stars …

## THE PIONEERS

### BILLY SHAW                    Offensive Lineman

• BORN: 12/15/1938    • PLAYED FOR TEAM: 1961 TO 1969

The Bills had a great running game in the 1960s, and Billy Shaw was the reason. He was fast enough to lead Buffalo's sweep and big enough to block two or three men on one play. Shaw played in eight **AFL All-Star Games** during his nine seasons.

### TOM SESTAK          Defensive Lineman

• BORN: 3/9/1936    • DIED: 4/3/1987
• PLAYED FOR TEAM: 1962 TO 1968

Tom Sestak was the most rugged defensive tackle in the AFL. He was a fearsome pass-rusher and one of the best at guessing an opponent's plays. "Big Ses" played most of his career with two injured knees and had to leave the sport before NFL fans got to see him play.

## COOKIE GILCHRIST — Running Back

- BORN: 5/25/1935   • PLAYED FOR TEAM: 1962 TO 1964

Cookie Gilchrist was a 250-pound running back who was impossible to stop when he got going. In his first season with the Bills, he became the first AFL player to rush for 1,000 yards. In the final game of the 1963 season, Gilchrist ran for 243 yards to set a new record.

## JACK KEMP — Quarterback

- BORN: 7/13/1935
- PLAYED FOR TEAM: 1962 TO 1967 & 1969

Jack Kemp was a great leader and one of the AFL's most athletic players. He led the Bills to three championship games in a row and was the league's **Most Valuable Player (MVP)** in 1965. He became a successful politician after football and ran for vice president of the United States in 1996.

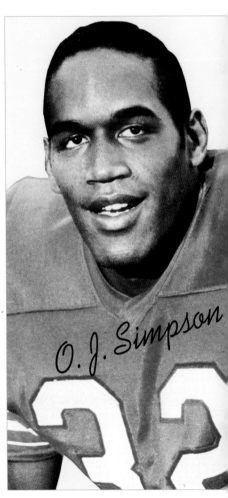

## O.J. SIMPSON — Running Back

- BORN: 7/9/1947   • PLAYED FOR TEAM: 1969 TO 1977

During his first three years with the Bills, O.J. Simpson did not get the ball nearly as often as he wanted. That changed in 1972, when the Bills rehired their old coach, Lou Saban. Saban gave Simpson the ball as often as he could. Over the next five years, the "Juice" led the NFL in rushing four times.

**LEFT**: Tom Sestak
**RIGHT**: O.J. Simpson

## FRED SMERLAS — Defensive Lineman

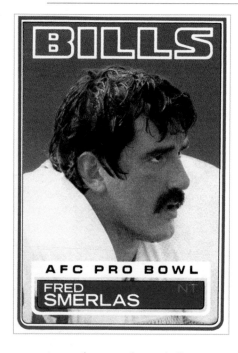

- BORN: 4/8/1957
- PLAYED FOR TEAM: 1979 TO 1989

Fred Smerlas was the anchor of the Bills' defensive line in the 1980s. He was voted to the **Pro Bowl** every year from 1980 to 1983 and again in 1988. Smerlas played nose tackle for most of his career and wrote a book about his life called *By a Nose*.

## ANDRE REED — Receiver

- BORN: 1/29/1964
- PLAYED FOR TEAM: 1985 TO 1999

Andre Reed was known for holding onto the ball after hard tackles and turning short passes into long plays. The speedy receiver led the AFC with 88 receptions in 1989. Reed caught 941 passes during his career for Buffalo.

## JIM KELLY — Quarterback

- BORN: 2/14/1960   • PLAYED FOR TEAM: 1986 TO 1996

Jim Kelly's teammates used to joke that he played quarterback like a linebacker. His toughness and talent helped the Bills reach the playoffs eight times in ten seasons. Kelly was a master of the "K-gun no-huddle" offense, barking out plays right at the line of scrimmage.

**LEFT**: Fred Smerlas
**TOP RIGHT**: Thurman Thomas
**BOTTOM RIGHT**: Bruce Smith

## THURMAN THOMAS     Running Back

• BORN: 5/16/1966    • PLAYED FOR TEAM: 1988 TO 1999

In most of the games he played in college and the NFL, Thurman Thomas was the best player on the field. He gained 1,000 yards eight years in a row and caught 50 or more passes in four different seasons. Thomas was the AFC's top rusher three times.

## BRUCE SMITH     Defensive Lineman

• BORN: 6/18/1963    • PLAYED FOR TEAM: 1985 TO 1999

Bruce Smith was the first choice in the 1985 **NFL draft**, and the Bills never made a better pick. Smith was the heart of Buffalo's defense. Though he was usually double-teamed or triple-teamed, Smith recorded 171 quarterback sacks with the Bills.

## LEE EVANS     Receiver

• BORN: 3/11/1981    • FIRST SEASON WITH TEAM: 2004

The Bills drafted Lee Evans so that their young quarterback, J.P. Losman, would have a target for his long passes. Evans gave the Bills the receiver they needed. In 2006, he led the team with 1,292 receiving yards and eight touchdown catches.

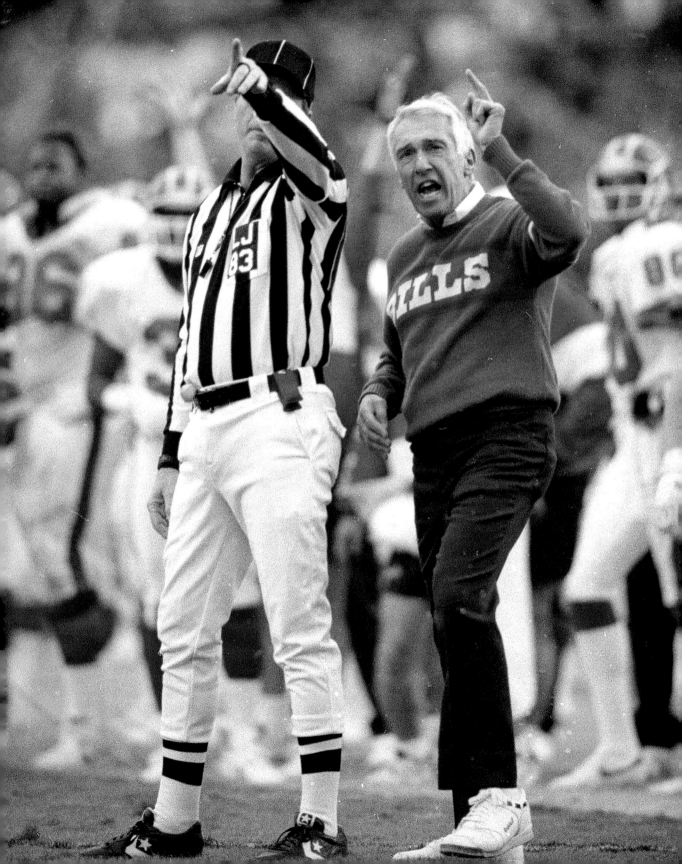

# On the Sidelines

The Bills have had three of history's best coaches working their sidelines. Lou Saban coached the team twice, from 1962 to 1965 and from 1972 to 1976. Saban matched quick and *agile* offensive linemen with big and fast running backs, such as Cookie Gilchrist and O.J. Simpson. He had just two losing seasons during his time with the Bills.

Chuck Knox coached the Bills for four seasons and led them to the playoffs twice. He believed in a strong defense and a powerful running game. The stars of his teams were quarterback Joe Ferguson and running back Joe Cribbs.

Marv Levy took the Bills to the Super Bowl four times. He designed a special offense that allowed his quarterback, Jim Kelly, to skip the huddle and call plays as he stood behind the center. This forced opponents to make *hasty* substitutions, which created opportunities for Kelly. Levy was also a believer in strong special teams. In many games, these part-time players made the difference between winning and losing.

Marv Levy always looked for a way to give the Bills an advantage. Here, he has a difference of opinion with an official.

# One Great Day

When the 1973 season started, Buffalo fans expected great things from the Bills. Their star running back, O.J. Simpson, did not disappoint them. In the first game of the year, he ran for 250 yards against the New England Patriots. By the season's seventh game, Simpson had reached 1,000 yards.

The record for most yards in a season at the time was 1,863. The great Jim Brown had set the mark 10 years earlier. Could O.J. beat it? With two games to go, Simpson had 1,584 yards. The Bills played the Patriots again, and he gained 219 yards. Now he was just 60 short of the record.

The Bills' final game was against the New York Jets. The Jets knew they could not keep Simpson from breaking the old record, but they **vowed** they would not let him reach 2,000 yards. At game time, it looked as if the weather would help them. It was a drizzly day, and the field was muddy and slick.

Simpson surprised the Jets and got off to a great start. In fact, he smashed Brown's record before the second quarter began. No matter what New York tried, Simpson found holes in the defense.

Late in the fourth quarter, he took a handoff from Joe Ferguson and followed blockers Reggie McKenzie and Mike Montler as they blasted a hole through the left side on the line. By the time the Jets brought Simpson down, he had gained seven yards. It gave him 200 for the game and 2,003 for the season. After a pressure-packed season and a hard-fought game, Simpson was asked how he felt to be the NFL's first 2,000-yard man. "Relieved," he smiled.

**LEFT**: O.J. Simpson    **ABOVE**: Simpson barrels through the New York defense on his record-breaking day.

# Legend Has It

## Who drove the hottest car on the Bills?

**LEGEND HAS IT** that Cookie Gilchrist did. Few fans had heard of Gilchrist when the Bills signed him. He did not play in college, and his only experience was in the **Canadian Football League**. That all changed in the summer of 1962, when he arrived at training camp. Gilchrist rolled into the parking lot in a bright red Cadillac convertible with gold letters stenciled on the side. They read "Lookie Lookie Here Comes Cookie."

**ABOVE:** Cookie Gilchrist **RIGHT:** Jack Kemp

# Was Jack Kemp the best bargain in team history?

**LEGEND HAS IT** that he was. In 1962, the Bills paid $100 for Kemp after the San Diego Chargers placed him on **waivers**. The quarterback had injured his finger, and San Diego needed his spot on the **roster** for another player. What a mistake. The Bills claimed Kemp, and he led them to two AFL Championship victories—over the Chargers!

**JACK KEMP**
QUARTERBACK

# Who made the biggest interception in Buffalo history?

**LEGEND HAS IT** that Carlton Bailey did—with help from Jeff Wright. In the third quarter of the 1991 AFC Championship game, the Bills and Denver Broncos were locked in a scoreless tie. The winner would go to the Super Bowl. With the ball on his own 19 yard line, Denver quarterback John Elway tried a **screen pass**. Wright guessed that this would be the play and was in position to tip the ball. Bailey caught it and ran past Elway for Buffalo's only touchdown of the day. The Bills held on to win 10–7.

# It Really Happened

The Bills' stadium can get very loud when Buffalo is winning. On January 3, 1993, it was deathly quiet. The 75,000 fans huddled in the stands that day for an AFC playoff game against the Houston Oilers were ready to surrender.

The second half had barely begun, and the Bills were way behind, 35–3. To make matters worse, three of their best players—Jim Kelly, Thurman Thomas, and Cornelius Bennett—were injured and on the bench. It looked like Buffalo's season was over.

Frank Reich, in at quarterback for Kelly, did not agree. He led the Bills on a touchdown drive to make the score 35–10. Next, the Bills surprised Houston and recovered an **onside kick**. Reich then threw a long touchdown pass to Don Beebe. When Buffalo got the ball back, Reich zipped a touchdown pass to Andre Reed. Suddenly, the crowd came alive.

After the Bills intercepted a pass, Reich and Reed connected in the end zone to make the score 35–31. Early in the fourth quarter, Reich hit Reed with another touchdown pass, and the Bills took the lead 38–35. When Houston tied the score with a last-second field goal, the game went into overtime.

The Buffalo crowd was louder than it had ever been as the sudden-death period began. The Oilers were completely *flustered* at that point. The stadium practically exploded when the Bills intercepted another pass. Moments later, Steve Christie kicked a 32-yard field goal for a 41–38 victory and the greatest comeback in the history of the playoffs.

**LEFT**: Keith McKeller raises a hand in celebration after a touchdown by Andre Reed against Houston.   **ABOVE**: Frank Reich and Steve Christie rejoice after the winning field goal in overtime.

# Team Spirit

**B**uffalo fans are loud and loyal. They have cheered the Bills to four Super Bowls and suffered with the team when it struggled. The city's oldest sports team has a special place in their hearts, and the stands in the Bills' stadium can be a very warm place—even on a freezing-cold day.

Actually, cold weather is something Bills fans know how to handle. They are also familiar with the big temperature swings that can take place on a Sunday in Buffalo. Fans come to the game dressed in layers. They are ready to peel off—or pack on—whatever is necessary to stay comfortable.

Many of these fans come from across the border, in Canada. The NFL has never placed a team in that country, which has its own football league. However, on any given Sunday, there are 15,000 or more fans from Canada cheering for the Bills. Many travel from as far as Toronto, which is three hours away, on the opposite side of Lake Ontario.

Willis McGahee gets a hug from the Buffalo fans after scoring a touchdown during a game in the 2004 season.

# Timeline

In this timeline, each Super Bowl is listed under the year it was played. Remember that the Super Bowl is held early in the year and is actually part of the previous season. For example, Super Bowl XLI was played on February 4th, 2007, but it was the championship of the 2006 NFL season.

**1960**
The Bills finish 5–8–1 in their first season.

**1973**
O.J. Simpson runs for 2,003 yards.

**1964**
The Bills win the AFL Championship.

**1977**
Joe Ferguson leads the AFC in passing yards and completions.

**1987**
Shane Conlan is named NFL Defensive **Rookie of the Year**.

The 1964 Buffalo Bills

Joe Ferguson

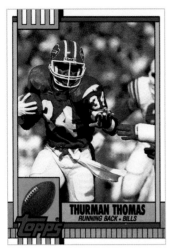

Thurman
Thomas

Bruce Smith, a
star on Buffalo's
Super Bowl teams.

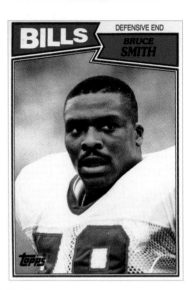

**1990**
James Lofton leads
the AFC with 20.3
yards per catch.

**1996**
Thurman Thomas
runs for 1,000 yards
for the eighth time.

**1998**
Steve Christie leads the
AFC with 140 points.

**1991**
Jim Kelly leads
the Bills to their
first Super Bowl.

**1994**
The Bills reach the
Super Bowl for the
fourth year in a row.

**2006**
Lee Evans scores
two 80-yard
touchdowns in
the same quarter.

Lee
Evans

# Fun Facts

## YOU GO LONG

In 1964, receiver Elbert Dubenion averaged an amazing 27.1 yards per

ELBERT DUBENION FLANKER BUFFALO BILLS

catch. No one with 40 or more catches has ever done better. Dubenion's nickname was "Golden Wheels."

## A LEG UP

When the Bills drafted Pete Gogolak in 1964, he became the first soccer-style kicker in pro football. In his first game for Buffalo, in the preseason against the New York Jets, he booted a 57-yard field goal. The record at the time was 56 yards.

## A MATTER OF TASTE

Cornelius Bennett was known in the NFL by his nickname, "Biscuit." As a child, Bennett could finish an entire plate of his mom's biscuits at one meal.

## YOU'RE FIRED! NO, YOU'RE HIRED!

In November 1964, Lou Saban waived Cookie Gilchrist after the two got into an argument. Gilchrist apologized, and Buffalo took him back. He ended up leading the AFL in rushing that season.

## ALL PROS

The Bills are Buffalo's fourth **professional** football team. The city's first team played in the NFL during the 1920s.

## FAMOUS FIRST

In 1969, James Harris opened the year as the Bills' quarterback. It marked the first time an African-American began a season as his team's starter at that position.

**He'll Ride the Plains of Civic Stadium**

HERE'S BUFFALO BILL, LOCAL AAC TEAM INSIGNIA

**LEFT**: Elbert Dubenion    **ABOVE**: A sketch of Buffalo's first mascot, which was introduced by the city's third pro team in 1947.

# Talking Football

"You've got to be more than a football player. You've got to be colorful. You've got to be a character!"

—*Cookie Gilchrist, on what made him stand out in a crowd*

"There's only one ball—we've got to keep it, and they've got to take it away."

—*Marv Levy, on not turning the ball over to your opponent*

"Every snap is like walking through an intersection during rush hour in Manhattan—with your eyes closed!"

—*Fred Smerlas, on what it was like to play nose tackle in the NFL*

"We were a particularly close team."

—*Billy Shaw, on the Buffalo teams of the 1960s*

"Some say I'm tough. Others say I'm just a big kid. The truth is that I'm a little of both."

—*Jim Kelly, on his love of a good, rough game*

"I wasn't the fastest or biggest guy around. I really liked football. I liked playing the game and competing."

—*George Saimes, on how he became an AFL All-Star*

"Every time I'm out there on the field, I'm trying to make something happen."

—*Thurman Thomas, on how he approached each play*

"I can't sleep after a game, whether we've won or lost, until I've studied the film, broken it down to find out how I played, and how we played as a unit."

—*Bruce Smith, on being a perfectionist*

**LEFT**: Marv Levy    **RIGHT**: Bruce Smith

# For the Record

The great Bills teams and players have left their marks on the record books. These are the "best of the best" …

## BILLS AWARD WINNERS

| WINNER | AWARD | YEAR |
|---|---|---|
| O.J. Simpson | Pro Bowl MVP | 1973 |
| O.J. Simpson | NFL Offensive Player of the Year | 1973 |
| O.J. Simpson | NFL Most Valuable Player | 1973 |
| Jim Haslett | NFL Defensive Rookie of the Year | 1979 |
| Chuck Knox | NFL Coach of the Year | 1980 |
| Shane Conlan | NFL Defensive Rookie of the Year | 1987 |
| Bruce Smith | Pro Bowl MVP | 1988 |
| Bruce Smith | NFL Defensive Player of the Year | 1990 |
| Thurman Thomas | NFL Offensive Player of the Year | 1991 |
| Thurman Thomas | NFL Most Valuable Player | 1991 |
| Jim Kelly | Pro Bowl MVP | 1991 |
| Steve Tasker | Pro Bowl MVP | 1993 |
| Bryce Paup | NFL Defensive Player of the Year | 1995 |
| Bruce Smith | NFL Defensive Player of the Year | 1996 |
| Doug Flutie | NFL Comeback Player of the Year | 1998 |

Shane Conlan

Bryce Paup

Doug Flutie

# BILLS ACHIEVEMENTS

| ACHIEVEMENT | YEAR |
| --- | --- |
| AFL East Champions | 1964 |
| AFL Champions | 1964 |
| AFL East Champions | 1965 |
| AFL Champions | 1965 |
| AFL East Champions | 1966 |
| AFC East Champions | 1980 |
| AFC East Champions | 1988 |
| AFC East Champions | 1989 |
| AFC East Champions | 1990 |
| AFC Champions | 1990 |
| AFC East Champions | 1991 |
| AFC Champions | 1991 |
| AFC Champions | 1992 |
| AFC East Champions | 1993 |
| AFC Champions | 1993 |
| AFC East Champions | 1995 |

Andre Reed and Cornelius Bennett, Pro Bowl players from the early 1990s.

Jim Kelly and Marv Levy, who led the Bills to four AFC Championships.

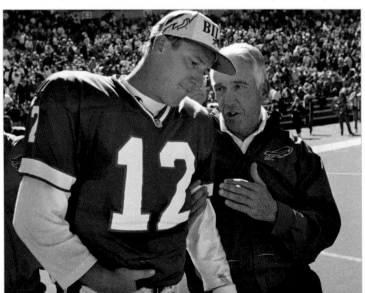

# Pinpoints

The history of a football team is made up of many smaller stories. These stories take place all over the map—not just in the city a team calls "home." Match the pushpins on these maps to the Team Facts and you will begin to see the story of the Bills unfold!

# TEAM FACTS

**1**    Buffalo, New York—*The Bills have played here since 1960.*

**2**    Pittsburgh, Pennsylvania—*Jim Kelly was born here.*

**3**    Norfolk, Virginia—*Bruce Smith was born here.*

**4**    Detroit, Michigan—*Reggie McKenzie was born here.*

**5**    Chicago, Illinois—*Marv Levy was born here.*

**6**    Vonore, Tennessee—*Mike Stratton was born here.*

**7**    Canton, Ohio—*George Saimes was born here.*

**8**    Lucedale, Mississippi—*Eric Moulds was born here.*

**9**    Houston, Texas—*Thurman Thomas was born here.*

**10**    Los Angeles, California—*Jack Kemp was born here.*

**11**    San Francisco, California—*O.J. Simpson was born here.*

**12**    Budapest, Hungary—*Pete Gogolak was born here.*

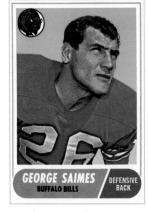

George Saimes

# Play Ball

Football is a sport played by two teams on a field that is 100 yards long. The game is divided into four 15-minute quarters. Each team must have 11 players on the field at all times. The group that has the ball is called the offense. The group trying to keep the offense from moving the ball forward is called the defense.

A football game is made up of a series of "plays." Each play starts and ends with a referee's signal. A play begins when the center snaps the ball between his legs to the quarterback. The quarterback then gives the ball to a teammate, throws (or "passes") the ball to a teammate, or runs with the ball himself. The job of the defense is to tackle the player with the ball or stop the quarterback's pass. A play ends when the ball (or player holding the ball) is "down." The offense must move the ball forward at least 10 yards every four downs. If it fails to do so, the other team is given the ball. If the offense has not made 10 yards after three downs—and does not want to risk losing the ball—it can kick (or "punt") the ball to make the other team start from its own end of the field.

At each end of a football field is a goal line, which divides the field from the end zone. A team must run or pass the ball over the goal line to score a touchdown, which counts for six points. After scoring a touchdown, a team can try a short kick for one "extra point," or try again to run or pass across the goal line for two points. Teams can score three points from anywhere on the field by kicking the ball between the goalposts. This is called a field goal.

The defense can score two points if it tackles a player while he is in his own end zone. This is called a safety. The defense can also score points by taking the ball away from the offense and crossing the opposite goal line for a touchdown. The team with the most points after 60 minutes is the winner.

Football may seem like a very hard game to understand, but the more you play and watch football, the more "little things" you are likely to notice. The next time you are at a game, look for these plays:

## PLAY LIST

**BLITZ**—A play where the defense sends extra tacklers after the quarterback. If the quarterback sees a blitz coming, he passes the ball quickly. If he does not, he can end up at the bottom of a very big pile!

**DRAW**—A play where the offense pretends it will pass the ball, and then gives it to a running back. If the offense can "draw" the defense to the quarterback and his receivers, the running back should have lots of room to run.

**FLY PATTERN**—A play where a team's fastest receiver is told to "fly" past the defensive backs for a long pass. Many long touchdowns are scored on this play.

**SQUIB KICK**—A play where the ball is kicked a short distance on purpose. A squib kick is used when the team kicking off does not want the other team's fastest player to catch the ball and run with it.

**SWEEP**—A play where the ball carrier follows a group of teammates moving sideways to "sweep" the defense out of the way. A good sweep gives the runner a chance to gain a lot of yards before he is tackled or forced out of bounds.

# Glossary

## FOOTBALL WORDS TO KNOW

**AFC CHAMPIONSHIP**—The game played to determine which AFC team will go to the Super Bowl.

**AFL ALL-STAR GAMES**—The exhibition games played between the top stars in the American Football League from 1962 to 1970.

**AFL CHAMPIONSHIP**—The game that decided the winner of the American Football League.

**ALL-AMERICA FOOTBALL CONFERENCE (AAFC)**—The professional league that played for four seasons, from 1946 to 1949.

**AMERICAN FOOTBALL CONFERENCE (AFC)**—One of two groups of teams that make up the National Football League. The winner of the AFC plays the winner of the National Football Conference (NFC) in the Super Bowl.

**AMERICAN FOOTBALL LEAGUE (AFL)**—The football league that began play in 1960 and later merged with the NFL.

**BLOCKERS**—Players who protect the ball carrier with their bodies.

**CANADIAN FOOTBALL LEAGUE**—A professional league in Canada that began play in 1958.

**DRAFT PICKS**—College players selected or "drafted" by NFL teams each spring.

**DRIVES**—Series of plays by the offense that "drive" the defense back toward its own goal line.

**EASTERN DIVISION**—A group of teams that play in the eastern part of the country. The Bills play in the AFC East.

**FIELD GOALS**—Goals from the field, kicked over the crossbar and between the goal posts. A field goal is worth three points.

**LINEMAN**—A player who begins each down crouched at the line of scrimmage.

**MOST VALUABLE PLAYER (MVP)**—The award given each year to the league's best player; also given to the best player in the Super Bowl and Pro Bowl.

**NATIONAL FOOTBALL LEAGUE (NFL)**—The league that started in 1920 and is still operating today.

**NFL DRAFT**—The annual meeting at which teams take turns choosing the best players in college.

**ONSIDE KICK**—A short kickoff that the kicking team tries to recover.

**PLAYOFF GAME**—A game played after the season to determine which teams play for the championship.

**PRO BOWL**—The NFL's all-star game, played after the Super Bowl.

**PROFESSIONAL**—A person or team that plays a sport for money. College players are not paid, so the are considered "amateurs."

**QUARTERBACK SNEAK**—A play in which the quarterback keeps the ball and tries to "sneak" past the defensive line.

**ROOKIE OF THE YEAR**—An award given each year to the best player in his first season.

**ROSTER**—The list of a team's active players.

**SCREEN PASS**—A short pass thrown to a player with a protective "screen" of blockers in front of him.

**SUPER BOWL**—The championship of football, played between the winners of the AFC and NFC.

**WAIVERS**—A list of players who have been released by their teams. A player appearing on this list has been "waived."

## OTHER WORDS TO KNOW

**AGILE**—Quick and graceful.

**BLUEPRINT**—A detailed plan used to build something.

**EXCEPTION**—Something left out or different from others in a group.

**FINANCE**—Contribute money to (a project).

**FLUSTERED**—Nervous and confused.

**HARD-NOSED**—Able to meet an opposition head-on.

**HASTY**—Quick and careless.

**MERGER**—A joining of two organizations.

**OVERWHELMED**—Defeated by a greater force.

**STRATEGIES**—Plans or methods for succeeding.

**TAILBONE**—The bone that protects the base of the spine.

**TIERS**—Levels of seats in a stadium.

**VOWED**—Made a serious promise.

---

# Places to Go

## ON THE ROAD

**BUFFALO BILLS**
One Bills Drive
Orchard Park, New York  14127
(716) 648-1800

**THE PRO FOOTBALL HALL OF FAME**
2121 George Halas Drive NW
Canton, Ohio  44708
(330) 456-8207

## ON THE WEB

**THE NATIONAL FOOTBALL LEAGUE**                    www.nfl.com
  • *Learn more about the National Football League*

**THE BUFFALO BILLS**                    www.buffalobills.com
  • *Learn more about the Buffalo Bills*

**THE PRO FOOTBALL HALL OF FAME**                    www.profootballhof.com
  • *Learn more about football's greatest players*

## ON THE BOOKSHELF

To learn more about the sport of football, look for these books at your library or bookstore:

  • Fleder, Rob–Editor. *The Football Book.* New York, NY: Sports Illustrated Books, 2005.

  • Kennedy, Mike. *Football.* Danbury, CT: Franklin Watts, 2003.

  • Savage, Jeff. *Play by Play Football.* Minneapolis, MN: Lerner Sports, 2004.

# Index

PAGE NUMBERS IN **BOLD** REFER TO ILLUSTRATIONS.

## The Team

**MARK STEWART** has written more than 20 books on football, and over 100 sports books for kids. He grew up in New York City during the 1960s rooting for the Giants and Jets, and now takes his two daughters, Mariah and Rachel, to watch them play in their home state of New Jersey. Mark comes from a family of writers. His grandfather was Sunday Editor of *The New York Times* and his mother was Articles Editor of *The Ladies' Home Journal* and *McCall's*. Mark has profiled hundreds of athletes over the last 20 years. He has also written several books about New York and New Jersey. Mark is a graduate of Duke University, with a degree in History. He lives with his daughters and wife Sarah overlooking Sandy Hook, New Jersey.

**JASON AIKENS** is the Collections Curator at the Pro Football Hall of Fame. He is responsible for the preservation of the Pro Football Hall of Fame's collection of artifacts and memorabilia and obtaining new donations of memorabilia from current players and NFL teams. Jason has a Bachelor of Arts in History from Michigan State University and a Master's in History from Western Michigan University where he concentrated on sports history. Jason has been working for the Pro Football Hall of Fame since 1997; before that he was an intern at the College Football Hall of Fame. Jason's family has roots in California and has been following the St. Louis Rams since their days in Los Angeles, California. He lives with his wife Cynthia and recent addition to the team Angelina in Canton, Ohio.